The Magical

1

Wheels & Stars

A Green Fire Folio

By
Coleston Brown

ISBN-13:   978-0986591266

Published in 2013 by

Le Brun Publications

Canada, Ireland

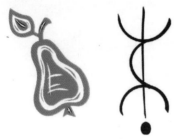

Cover art and design

by Coleston Brown

Book design by Coleston Brown

A Green Fire Folio on the
Magical Way

Contents

Preface and Acknowledgments

As with much else in my magical career the seeds of my work with the Magical Tree were first planted by Gareth Knight many years ago in 1978, when I learned from him how to draw the Tree of Life using three intersecting circles or wheels. It was about the same time that I came across a drawing of a Three Wheeled Tree in an 18th century chapbook of Rosicrucian teachings (see Figure 6 below) and was first inspired to investigate this particular form of the Tree, which seemed to be a remnant of something earlier and more primal than the conventional forms of the Tree of Life as presented by most of the Qabalistically trained pundits of the day. It was Gareth Knight too, who introduced me to the work of one of his own teachers, William G. Gray, who suggested a pattern of Three Wheels on the Tree in several of his books. Mr. Knight also first introduced me to the writings of R.J. Stewart. Despite his way of rendering the Tree of Life from intersecting circles, to my knowledge Gareth Knight never developed the Tree in terms of Three Wheels; William Gray seems only to have touched on the pattern implicitly; while Mr. Stewart, a respected teacher and writer in his own right, seems to have developed an approach of his own from Gray's initial insights (*see* , in particular, Stewart's books *The Miracle Tree*, 2003, and *The Merlin Tarot, 1991*) . As will be discovered in the pages that follow, my own views and approach are quite divergent from those of these other writers, although I acknowledge their influence in helping to spark my own realisations on the subject.

Thanks are due to all those who read and commented on the material presented here during its long period of development, in particular Robert Whiteside, Laurel Bohart, Rab Wilkie, and Marina Romero. João Claudio Fuentes, And to those unnamed who helped in untold ways: Thank-you! Many thanks also to Cliff and Pauline McClinton, and also to "Twilight and "the Pixie" for ongoing support and encouragement. And of Course, heart-felt acknowledgment to my lady, Faery Artist Jessie Skillen, for much support and helpful advice on the design and inclusion of images, including several of her own wonderful creations.

The Folio you are holding is a unique and original work based on decades of study and experience and it is my sincere hope that these writings on the Magical Tree will help students of the Esoteric and Magical Arts, no matter what their level of knowledge and experience. Those new to the subject will gain a valuable tool for spiritual development and service, whereas those versed in more conventional forms of the Tree will find here much that will "cut to the chase," so to speak, revealing and preserving the essential core of the tradition and its roots in the spiritual perceptions and experiences of the ancients.

 I suggest reading the entire folio through at least once before trying any of the practices.

Carrowreagh, County Sligo, Éire— 2013

What is the Magical Tree?

The Magical Tree is a tool for deep spiritual training and work, and is a core component of the Magical Way.

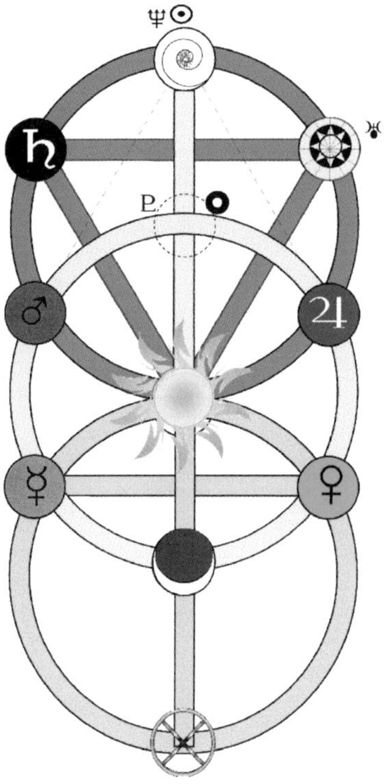

The roots of the Magical Tree run through many layers of world tradition and sacred lore. This includes such diverse areas as archaic Shamanic practice, Vedic traditions of the *skhamba*, Mesopotamian Tree Mysteries, and ancient Celtic and European World Tree images (the latter epitomised by the Norse Yggdrasil). But contemporary esoteric students perhaps best recognise it as an aspect of Qabala.[1]

Qabala & Shamanism

Qabala is a form of Jewish esotericism that focuses on the mystical interpretation of scripture and the divine attributes or "emanations" of God. Qabala incorporates diagrams of a stylised Tree known as the Sephirotic Tree, and often identified with the biblical Tree of Paradise. A set of named and numbered spheres or circles (the *sephiroth*), and a series of interconnecting lines or "paths", are used to represent it.

Figure 1: Basic form of the Magical Tree. Coleston Brown 2013

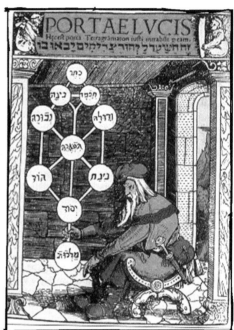

Figure 2: **Shamanic apparel and accoutrements often sport images of the Cosmic tree , the planets and stars. In some traditions,the tree image was also an icon of the goddess and mirrored a carved figure that formed the drum handle on the back. Above: Artist's rendering of an Altaic shaman's drum ,1924 (see also Figure 5 below.)**

Figure 3:The Jewish mystical Tradition of Qabala conceptualised ancient images and perceptions of the Cosmic tree. These conceptualisations were rendered diagrammatically as the Sephirotic Tree of which one version is shown above. From a LAtin translation by Paulus Ricius of Portae Lucis by Joseph Gikatilla (1248 -1325) Augsburg, 1516

The general design of this glyph is similar to early Mesopotamian varieties of the Sacred Tree pattern, which was likely introduced from central Asia where it is still prominent in Shamanic initiation and practice.[2]

Recent scholarship suggests that a basic pattern similar to the Sephirotic Tree was already well developed in

Figure 4 The design of the conventional Sephirotic Tree is likely a development of Mesopotamian Sacred Tree Images such as that illustrated above. From a cylinder seal: The king in the form of a sacred bird, mediates the divine streams.

Mesopotamia in the fourth millennium BCE.

By the time of the Babylonian Exile (ca 587 BCE), when many foreign mystical concepts and ideas became firmly ensconced in Judaic experience, the Tree pattern would have acquired a relatively fixed and formal design.[3]

Qabala was seized upon by proselytising Christians in the late Middle Ages and used as a pernicious weapon for

Figure 5 magic poles are used by shamans in many archaic cultures as supports for visions through the spiritual layers of the cosmos The birds signify the shaman's skill at magical flight.

converting Jews. One hopes that in the midst of this there were also Christians who studied Qabala for its spiritual value. Unfortunately, evidence of this is scarce. The tradition was actively stirred in the Renaissance when Pico della Mirandola presented his 900 theses in Rome It then

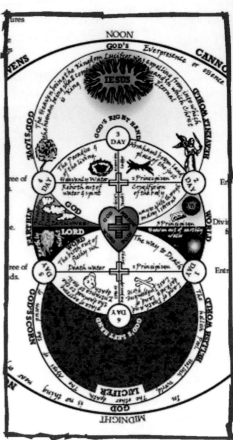

Figure 6: Rosicrucian Tradition, which in part derives from Ancient European Faery Lore preserved a "Three Wheels" version of the Magical Tree. 1785

gradually died out from public notice, though not before being taken up in the influential works of people like Cornelius Agrippa, Knorr von Rosenroth and the English Rosicrucian, Robert Fludd.[4]

Qabala was rediscovered in the nineteenth century by European occultists who adopted certain elements of Jewish and Christian Qabala, including a particular version

of the Tree diagram (earlier Jewish and Christian Qabala had many versions). Unfortunately for most contemporary magical practitioners, the Tree has remained mired in rigid cultural viewpoints deriving from early twentieth-century fraternities such as the Hermetic Order of the Golden Dawn and its descendents.

A universal magical Form

Fortunately, this series of folios on the Magical Tree is not about Qabala. For although Qabala preserved several variants of an archaic Tree pattern within its complex doctrines, the Magical Tree is a universal magical form and can not be identified with, or restricted to, a few currents of religious or esoteric tradition.[5]

This does not invalidate the more conventional contexts of the Magical Tree — clearly many still gain insight, comfort and security from them — but it does put them into perspective.

The Magical Tree is an enduring, organic pattern of universal powers, presences and planetary cycles. It has wide-ranging applications to personal development and spiritual transformation, applications that extend into the areas of planetary stewardship and environmental care. It is a living pattern, which, when integrated into our daily experience, deepens and expands awareness of the nature of reality.

The Components of the Magical Tree

There are three key elements underpinning the design of the Magical Tree:

i) The Three Wheels

The forms and rhythms which generate the essential framework of the Magical Tree fall naturally into three rotational patterns or Wheels (*see esp. Figures 1, 6, 7-9 & pages 14-15*):

1. **The Stellar Wheel, centred on the Void.**

2. **The Solar Wheel, centred on the Sun.**

3. **The Lunar Wheel, centred on the Moon**

These Three Wheels interlace to form the activating structure of the Magical Tree. They are linked to cosmic rhythms of the Sun, Moon and Stars. In the diagram of the Tree, they are represented by three intersecting circles along a central line or axis. (*Figure 1*). The Three Wheels are the basis for experiencing and understanding the flow of spiritual forces or energies around the Tree.

The model of the Three Wheels arises naturally through participation in the primordial rhythms of life and is thus far older than any written source. The Three Wheels are a simple and direct model of the universe as a living holism, a Living Magical Tree, that places us on Earth in wholesome relation to, Sun, Moon and Stars, and attunes us to their transformational rhythms and energies. It is telling that establishment occultists, esotericists, and spiritual teachers are generally unaware of the vibrant and essential pattern underlying the Tree. But it is perhaps typical of both conventional spirituality and orthodox occultism to lose contact with vital inner structures and spiritual rhythms. (*Figure 7*).

✦ ✦ ✦ ✦ ✦ ✦

ii) The Planets/Spheres

The concept of spheres is closely connected to the traditional teaching that the sun, moon and five ancient planets or "wandering stars" signify or demarcate planes or levels of being. In the ancient world, the planets were associated with the "heavenly spheres," which could be traversed in vision by mystics and initiates. The Spheres on the Tree should be approached as fields of

A

The stellar wheel, centred on the void and pivot (pole star)

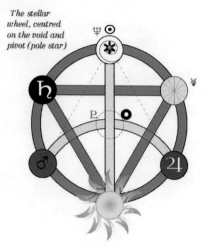

influence or energy, and not little circles or balls, even though we draw or represent them diagrammatically as circles or balls, and even occasionally envision them that way in magical work. They have no "place" per se,

that resonates and relates with innumerable images, experiences and forms.

There is also a non-sphere, signified by a dotted circle and associated with the Void, the Unknown or Mystery, which is imageless and formless yet central to the dynamics of the Tree. (*Figures 7 & 8*).

B *The solar wheel, centred on the sun.*

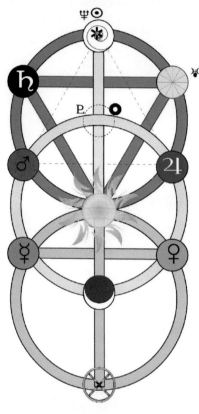

iii) Paths

Depicted as lines between pairs of Spheres, the twenty-two Paths comprise the Third Component of the Magical Tree. The Paths function in two main modalities (*Figures 7 & 8*):

1. **as a fusion of the powers of the Spheres they connect.**

2. **as pathways or channels between Spheres.**

C *The lunar wheel, centred on the moon.*

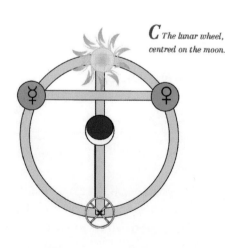

Figure 8. The ten "spheres" and the Twenty-two "paths" associated with earth, moon, sun and stars, (including the 5 "wandering stars" of the ancients, i.e., the planets)

only relationships. The Ten Spheres are truly fields of energy and consciousness, each emanating from a core of regenerative spiritual power

Either way, whether directly assuming them into consciousness or walking them in vision, we are mediating between primal powers, enabling or allowing them to co-mingle within our being and to be expressed in our experience.

Figure 7 A-C The Three Wheels shown individually.

It will be noted that the Magical Tree is largely about

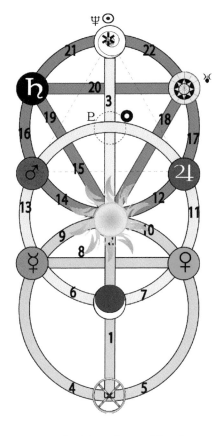

Figure 9 . The 22 Paths. Unlike the conventional Qabalistc tree (figures13-14) the Magical Tree retains the wheel structure, so the paths are mainly curved.(numbers are for reference only)

experience, about participating in primal powers of regeneration and illumination. Reading about the Tree is merely a preparation or follow-up to experience. The Tree is not an intellectual puzzle, a description of God (God taken as proper name, thus capitalised), the gods, or the universe, and it certainly is

not a "filing system" or primitive computer. Nothing could be further from reality.

Functions & Characteristics

There are a number of important functions and characteristics of the Magical Tree

1) **Sacred Presences**.
In spiritual traditions sacred

Figure 10: The Dundon Yew. The Yew is a tree sacred in Celtic and faery traditions, where it often signifies the cosmic axis and thus a sacred liminal place where passage between Realms and Worlds is enabled and where healing and harmony may be encountered. Photo courtesy Robert Henry.

trees not only mark holy places of power, they are indwelt by sacred presences, by ancestors, spirits or divinities. A famous cave painting at Lascaux, France clearly represents a kind of magical tree vision: a bird-headed or masked human figure lies on the ground while nearby a bird perches on a pole or tree. The bird is likely the "power being," or personal / tribal guardian spirit, dwelling in the Sacred Tree. Other prehistoric tree images show that trees and plants in general were connected with sacred beings sprung from the Earth or Star Mother.

In Mesopotamian iconography, Tree images are often stylised and are almost always identified or associated with gods and goddesses.

The later Qabalistic or Sephirotic Tree pends from these early shamanic and Mesopotamian models, with the various divinities replaced by attributes of a masculine creator, though other aspects, whether androgynous as in the archangels and angels or abstractly feminine as in the Shekinah, also remain or develop.

This is not to suggest a simplistic "diffusionist" evolution of the glyph of the Magical Tree. Undoubtedly in some instances the tree glyph was adopted, absorbed and integrated through invasion or trade, in other cases there was likely an independent or

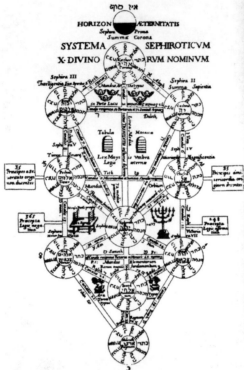

Figure 11. from a 17th century work by Atanasius Kircher influenced generations of Occult Qabalists who adopted the same pattern of paths or channels linking pairs of Spheres. Although obviously deriving from the 3-wheel pattern found in the Rosicrucian and faery traditions which form the inspiration for the Magical tree pattern as presented in this folio, the rotational element was quickly lost and supplanted by more linear patterns of 1eighteenth and nineteenth Century Occultism, dominate the thinking and practice of most magical students today. See also pp14-15 below: Drawing the Magical Tree

Figure 12: a modern rendition of the tree with paths in accordance with Kircher's arrangement.

spontaneous manifestation of a spiritual Form. All sacred trees tend toward, but never fulfil on their own, the reality of the Universal Tree.

2) The Living Tree.

For many contemporary people, raised on the assumptions of post-Cartesian dualism, the idea of the material world as a living being is hard to grasp. Yet this

In an early Irish cycle of legends the faery man Fer Fi is said to have created a magic Yew Tree at Samhain, that, as the Poem says, " was not a tree but a fairy vision, its type does not exist." The Tree was conjured in response to a break in human-faery relations brought about by misdeeds of the legendary Irish king Aileel. although the tree could offer "protection against every harm," it was also the source of dispute and division for those who were greedy or covetous. This sacred tree is "hidden secretly by the elves (i.e. Faery) with mysterious control" and can be discovered by few.

Clearly we have here a depiction of a cosmic tree originating in and protected by Faery. It is depicted as liminal and enchanted, greatly desired by humans, but dangerous to those of ill will or impure motive.

Figure 13 Above is a detail from the North High Cross at Aheny, depicting Fer Fi on the left with his tiompan (ancient celtic zither) beneath the Magic Yew Tree.

Source: The Yew of the Disputing Sons: by Myles Dillon Ériu, Vol. 14 (1946), pp. 154-165

is precisely the primary significance of the Magical Tree in many ancient spiritual traditions.

We are part of an organism ~ a universal living being ~ and when we encounter living trees we are able to gain access to universal mysteries. This is because trees participate in and reflect, in a

Figure 14: In this Palaeolithic cave painting from the famed Lascaux cave in France, a shamanic figure lies in trance, Near him is a pole with a bird, probably signifying the world tree and cosmic axis which joins the mortal world and Otherworld and enables visionary travel between them. Bird Shaman, Lascaux circa 17000 BP

special way, the living cosmic structure. A tree, with its roots below, its leaves, flowers and fruit above and its central trunk carrying life-giving fluid in-between, easily assimilates the ancient three-fold vision of the world as comprised of Three Realms: Sky, Earth and under-earth. These are not merely the commonly understood material or

physical regions, but integrated visions of universal patterns that harmonise material and spiritual aspects of reality. Subjective and objective are fused ~ though not indistinct. The Three Realms are experience both in the Natural, Physical World and in the OtherWorld of spiritual Power and Presence.

The Magical Tree is organic. It changes and grows. It has rhythm ~ something that has been missed almost entirely in Modern approaches to it, which tend to constrict or fossilise that which is vital and flowing. There are lunar, solar, planetary and stellar rhythms or wheels under which we all live, and by which we are all affected, even though they are often overlaid and obscured by the artificial rhythms and light sources of modern civilisation. Part of living the Magical Tree is to consciously reconnect with these primal rhythms and cycles. They are the key to much, as they express revolutions of being, becoming, and regeneration.

3) Holism.

The Magical Tree not only represents and embodies the Worlds, Realms, Presences and Powers, it links them together in relationships. The Magical Tree expresses relationship. It is a holism.

The Magical Tree is a glyph of total reality, of all that proceeds from the Source and is encompassed, expressed and permeated by it. Our perceptions of reality are incomplete. We live in a fragmented world alienated from the Real. This is part reflection, part cause ~ for the two are inseparably joined ~ of our own sense of incompleteness as human beings. Our instinctive quest for wholeness, whether followed out in the banal seeking after material "happiness," the pursuit of romantic love, or in a magico-spiritual search for enlightenment, provides motivation for life above the subsistence level.

In world mythology we have the quest for the tree, plant or fruit of immortality (which includes the drink made from these such as the elixir of life, ambrosia, hoama, soma, etc.) All such trees, plants, foods, and so on, are significant fragments that reveal a whole that is greater than themselves. This is the holism of the Magical Tree.

Wholeness is often expressed as a sphere. Indeed there are early esoteric traditions which depict the Universal Magical Tree as a sphere. Most anciently this was imaged in the intersections of the Milky Way, the circle of the horizon, and the solstitial and equinoctial colures. Comparatively recent (ca 200-600 AD) is an anonymous document known as the Book of Formation,[6] which describes the creation of the universe in terms of a three-ring sphere, though this was tellingly mis-imaged as a square box by early twentieth-century occultists and their spiritual descendants.

In contemporary magical practice, we study, experience and work the Tree patterns in order to restore broken relationships, first in ourselves, and through this, in accordance with the principle of harmonic resonance, onto deeper communal, collective and planetary levels.

4) Spiritual Orientation

Most obviously, however, the holistic power of the Magical Tree is seen in its role as universal axis. In world spiritual traditions, the universal axis unites the Three Realms. It is the place where access is gained to the various levels of reality and it provides a means of ingress and egress to and from those levels. Another way of putting this is to say that our relationship with the structure of the Tree provides a means of inner orientation, a clearly defined way of initiation or self transformation.

The Magical Tree embodies a way of attuning to reality on several levels. It is on one hand a way of psychological orientation, and on another a way of orienting towards objective inner or spiritual reality. It also aligns the physical body to flows and centres of magical power.

Psychologically, the Tree helps us understand ourselves and the psychic processes and issues that dominate our internal dialogue, selfworth, relationships and sense of place in the world. It is thus a tool for reestablishing and maintaining psychic balance. This is a function of its properties as a holism.

*Figure 16:*The folktale *Jack and the Beanstalk* seems to be formed upon remnants of ancient traditions of the Magical Tree as cosmic axis and point of access to various worlds and realms

Figure 17: The ladder sometimes becomes a substitute for the Magical Tree. In the Mithraic Mysteries, for instance ,it functions much as the tree/pole does in Shamanic practice and initiation
Above: a bas relief of the Mithraic mysteries with mystic ladder on the right. Each rung represented a degree of initiation and a Stellar Realm or constellation

Figure 18: "Taking one of the stones of the place, he put it under his head and lay down in that place to sleep. And he dreamed, and behold, there was a ladder set up on the earth, and the top of it reached to heaven; and behold, the angels of God were ascending and descending on it!" This description of Jacob's ladder appears in Genesis 28:10-19, An interesting connection is that Bethel, where Jacob's dream takes place, is associated with Luz, a legendary underground city of immortals that was reached by entering a cleft in a tree. In the painting above,William Blake, who was conversant with the Western Esoteric Tradition, depicts Jacob's ladder as a spiral stair, thus fusing several important magical forms.

How to draw the Magical Tree

a. make a line, divided it into two equal sections

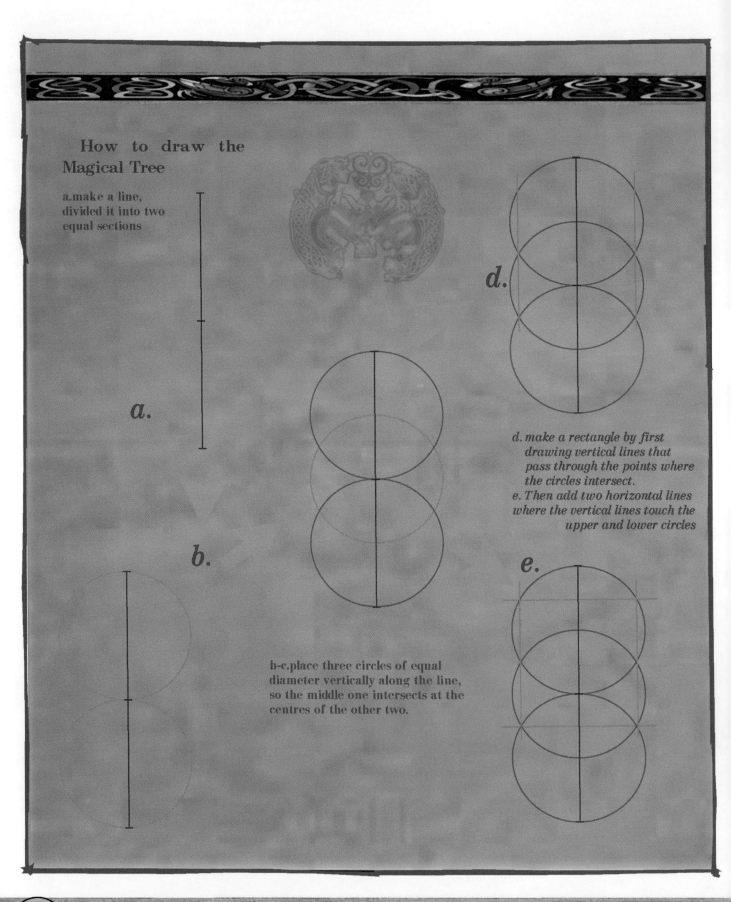

a.

b.

b-c. place three circles of equal diameter vertically along the line, so the middle one intersects at the centres of the other two.

d.

d. make a rectangle by first drawing vertical lines that pass through the points where the circles intersect.

e. Then add two horizontal lines where the vertical lines touch the upper and lower circles

e.

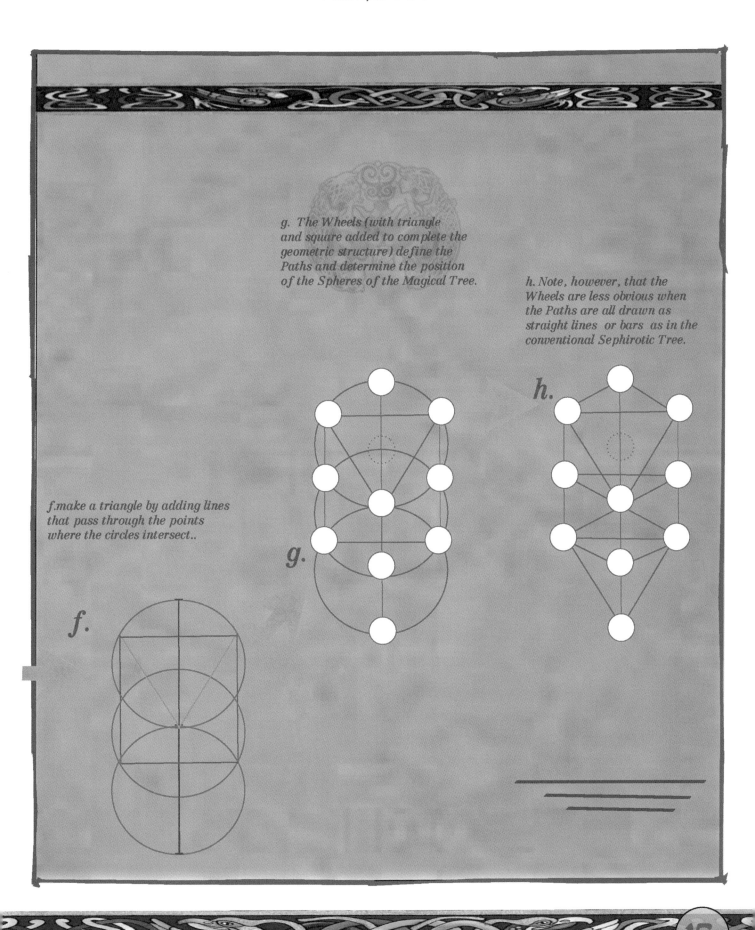

g. The Wheels (with triangle and square added to complete the geometric structure) define the Paths and determine the position of the Spheres of the Magical Tree.

h. Note, however, that the Wheels are less obvious when the Paths are all drawn as straight lines or bars as in the conventional Sephirotic Tree.

f. make a triangle by adding lines that pass through the points where the circles intersect..

g.

h.

f.

On a spiritual level, the Magical Tree provides a means of approaching the depths of reality. It is a map of the Realms, a guide for pilgrims and travellers in the Otherworld. It teaches us that when we move in a certain direction we can expect to meet certain kinds of experiences.

The Tree can be climbed, or descended vertically, it can also be experienced radiantly ~ out from the centre ~ or horizontally. From a purely physical standpoint, humans and trees share a unique, radiant verticality, which is most simply expressed in

terms of a model of seven directions. No one direction is a correct one, each has its own tonality or keynote and all are valid means of experiencing magical realities and spiritual realms.

In some Shamanic traditions, a sacred tree or notched pole, representing the multileveled cosmos, is climbed during initiation (and often thereafter) as a means of orienting and mediating a spiritual vision. The shaman will climb to a certain level marked by a branch or notch of the pole and, stopping there, describe the corresponding aspect of the Otherworld. This

ascent is normally accompanied by a drum made of a wood associated with the Cosmic Tree.

Recent discoveries on the northeastern coast of England reveal interesting perspectives on the Magical Tree of the Celts (or pre-Celts): At the centre of a ring of prehistoric timbers a great oak stump was inverted. This is clearly a physical anchor for the inverted Tree of the UnderRealm, which is descended (in vision) rather than ascended (c.f. Figure 19).

This kind of operational image is not limited to Shamanic or Celtic practices either, Mithraic initiates climbed a ladder (a substitute or development of the Tree image) representing initiatory grades, sacred metals and planetary or stellar regions.

Just as the physical trees of shamans, Celtic tribal wizards, and magi allowed them to orient the worlds and maintain a course in the maze of the inner realms, so do contemporary practitioners of the Magical Way use a virtual tree ~ a tree pattern impressed into consciousness, drawn, studied, visioned, modelled, identified with ~ to orient and stay their course in the OtherWorld. All in a sense, if by differing means, "become" the Tree.

Figure 19: SeaHenge. The notion of a tree linking the Worlds and Realms is highlighted in the significance of this early Bonze-age oak-post timber circle commonly known as Seahenge. Seahenge is remarkable in that the centre of the circle is occupied by an inverted oak stump, which forms a kind of altar or ritual platform. The inverted tree growing in the underworld links closely with the celtic or pre-celtic emphasis on the mysteries of ancestors and other sacred presences in the

Figure 20: Celtic Menhirs and Shamanic Deer stones (inset) function much the same as the Magical Tree in that they are images of the axis and as such provide access to other worlds, Realms and Beings.

Figure 21: Mist flows over the dark plain where a lone standing stone awaits the awakening of the land.   in the foreground a faery horn hangs from a enchanted tree. When sounded, the horn will awaken the land causing it to green out into a vision of *Magh Mel*, the "Honeyed Plain" — an otherworldly place often encountered in Faery Lore. *The Star* painted in 2008, by Coleston Brown

5) Regeneration

Because the Magical Tree is a means of orientation and passage between the Realms, it is also a pattern of initiatory experience. Initiation in all world traditions deals with regeneration of consciousness, and often of physical vitality, through an enactment, explicit or implicit, of death, regeneration and rebirth. In universal terms this pattern is threefold: powerful UnderRealm and OverRealm encounters are mediated into the Mundane Realm of incarnation and physical reality. The threefold pattern easily extends into seven (by adding four Elements or four horizontal directions) or Ten (by further circulating a triangle of three vessels or powers around the centre ~ a much misunderstood ritual form once known as "the Triangle of Art").

We will be dealing practically with various sacred powers in the course of these folios on the Magical Tree, learning to work with them, to relate to what they are and what they evoke within us. We will, in effect, be consecrating our consciousness, indeed our very being, by directing our selves to think, feel and live in accord with the Magical Tree. The process of being the Tree is similar to the process familiar

Figure 22: **The concepts of rebirth and renewal are commonly found in Celtic and Faery Lore The endless contest between Bright and Shadow as the wheel of the seasons turns is deeply resonant with the regenerative power of the Magical Tree. Above,** *The Holly King and The Oak King* **painting by Jessie Skillen**

to musicians whereby they identify on a deep soul level with their instruments. Thus their instruments become an extension of their being, which allows them true expression. There is much similarity between magic and music. In order to live the Tree we must first tune ourselves by setting our intention in a certain direction, the direction of wholeness and regenerated Being.

6) Resonance

This is the property or quality that interweaves various influences not only within a specific Wheel, Sphere or Path, but also among the Wheels, Spheres and Paths themselves. Resonance is the magical linking or connecting principle. It is what enables us to recognise and respond to attributes or associations among magical forms.

For instance, **Avalon**, the name of the legendary Blessed Isle of Britain, is related to a

Celtic word for apple *Abal*. The Isle of Avalon is connected in Arthurian Tradition to Glastonbury, Somerset. (The 12th century Latin Chronicler Gerald of Wales calls Glastonbury "the Isle of Apples").[7] The apple tree, being so closely associated with the spiritual centre of Britain, assumes the role of World Tree and cosmic axis. Anyone who has cut an apple in half knows that the seed chambers are in the form of a five-pointed star. The five rayed star or pentagram becomes, in this case, a core image or pattern of the Avalonian tradition. It can effectively be incorporated into rituals, meditations and journeys, or customised into ritual objects and paraphernalia relating to the Avalonian way.

Now, on the Universal Tree, the pentagram resonates with Sphere Five, which expresses a power connected with the element of Fire that works through the principle of removal or opening. Pentagrams have often been used in rituals for releasing influences (banishing) or opening doors to inner realms, and could be effective in opening rites relating to Avalon (we could link this to "the Flaming Door" of Celtic tradition).

This is the principle of Resonance at work, it allows us to recognise meaningful, magical connections among various forms, experiences and events. Resonance is thus central to magical work, which rests on the generation of appropriate forms and patterns for the mediation of spiritual power.

*****

Of Wandering Stars & Spinning Wheels

Knowledge of the stars, including what the ancients called "the Wandering Stars" ~sun, moon and planets~ is crucial for our understanding of the Magical Tree. Such Knowledge might be termed *Primal Star Lore* [8].

I have chosen the term *Primal Star Lore* to distinguish the subject from both materialist astronomy, which merely measures and theorises, and modern astrology, which rarely goes beyond a superficial and secondary

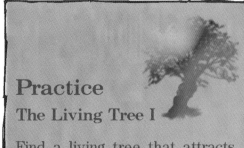

Practice
The Living Tree I

Find a living tree that attracts you and is accessible (obviously a tree behind a fence on a neighbour's property will not usually work, unless your neighbours are sympathetic). Seek to commune with the tree: touch the tree, feel its living presence, spend a little time with it and feel a bond with it like you would with an old friend whom you haven't seen in many years. Be aware of the powers of the tree. Especially at this time, be aware of its power to join the Realms and grant access to them, ask the tree to share these powers with you. Give a small amount of water as an offering of friendship.

Practice
The Living Tree II

Continue to build your connection with the living presence of the Tree by envisioning it in meditation. You do not need to be near the physical tree to connect with it. Once you have formed your bond, you carry the relationship within you wherever you are. Touch it in vision with your inner senses as you did with your physical senses in the outer realm. Build an image of the Tree in your inner vision. At first this will likely be similar to the physical appearance of the Tree, but with experience, you will find the Tree take on a more fluid form and will change, grow and transform before you. The Tree will tend to take on magical properties (for instance it is common for a tree to appear with leaves of living green flame — emphasising its connection to the OtherWorld of Faery that rests behind our physical reality).

understanding of star forms and the rhythms of time, space, and event. Primal Astronomy is a way of knowing through experience, through participation in the life of the universe.

The West's inheritance of Greek and Roman names for star patterns and planets has led most magical practitioners to seek their initial understanding of star forms in Greco-Roman mythology. Now, the study of myth and legend is indispensable for magical work and is a great adjunct to the experience of Primal Astronomy. However, as long as we take the Greco-Roman or any other mythological system as our starting point for understanding the stars and planets, we are operating at levels at least once-removed from experiential reality.

For instance, the planet Mercury is usually approached by studying and meditating on the attributes and characteristics of Mercury, the Roman god of commerce, travel and communication. If the student is lucky there may be a consideration of other related mythological figures such as the Greek Hermes, Babylonian Nabu, Celtic Artaios, etc. Unfortunately, while this approach might

introduce the student to Roman or comparative mythology, it teaches little about the magical significance of the planet itself, its rhythms and movements in the sky and what they mean.

Primal or Sacred Star Lore interests itself mainly in the interactions of the Earth, Sun, Moon, Stars (the Milky Way and the 42 ancient constellations) and the five ancient (visible) planets or wandering stars, which have played an important and enduring role in magical traditions for millennia. Less attention is paid to the planets Uranus, Neptune and Pluto (♅, ♆, ♇),none of which were known before the discovery of Uranus in the late seventeenth century ~ and no attention is given to the modern constellation groups devised since the early 20th century as an aid to the researches of materialist astronomy.

The issue is one of direct primary participation rather than secondary intellectualisation. It is therefore crucial to recognise that Primal Astronomy is not about observing distant phenomena, but about experiencing the living universe. Now this doesn't mean that to participate in cosmic rhythms you must

retire to a mountaintop and contemplate the heavens. But if you are going to work effectively in Magic, you do need to become aware of these rhythms and to consciously tune yourself to them. Many realisations about the Sun, Moon and Stars may be gained from a balcony in an urban apartment complex, from backyard meditations or from a sunrise, moonrise or star-rise seen on an open stretch of road.

Like all primal magical patterns, starforms are experienced simply and directly. They are not particularly complicated, confusing or difficult to understand. They only become so when we lose touch with the living universe ~ the Living Tree ~ and identify with abstractions or intellectual overlays that are disconnected from the very realities they are meant to elucidate, express or expand upon.

The starforms fuse with the Ten Powers of the Tree (*see Figure 1*). They are one of several types of energies or influences that co-mingle to generate the Spheres. Before looking at the way starforms are expressed rhythmically in the Three Wheels, it will be useful to consider the earth and Stars as our ancient

ancestors would have experienced them.

Figure 1

10 The Earth Star

Primal Star Lore interlaces with spiritual cosmology ~ how the universe is patterned or structured spiritually, That is, with the Three Realms[9] and the Two Worlds. [10]

Primal Star Lore is expressed in the Three Realms and two Worlds as follows:

i) Above in the OverRealm, where astro-events are observed in the sky and intersect with life in the atmosphere and on the surface of the planet.

ii) Below in the UnderRealm where astro-events, powers, rhythms, cycles extend below the horizon or beneath the Earth and become active by shining through or from within the land.

iii) In-between, in the MidRealm where cycles, rhythms and powers become active within living things, the creatures in the landscape, the atmosphere, and the surface of the Earth.

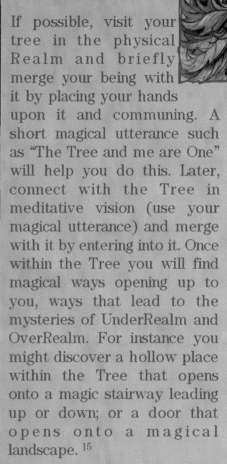

Practice
The Living Tree III

If possible, visit your tree in the physical Realm and briefly merge your being with it by placing your hands upon it and communing. A short magical utterance such as "The Tree and me are One" will help you do this. Later, connect with the Tree in meditative vision (use your magical utterance) and merge with it by entering into it. Once within the Tree you will find magical ways opening up to you, ways that lead to the mysteries of UnderRealm and OverRealm. For instance you might discover a hollow place within the Tree that opens onto a magic stairway leading up or down; or a door that opens onto a magical landscape. [15]

This is a deep and potent magical exercise and should not be confused with New Age tree hugging or other tepid activities that trivialise the ancient spiritual bond between humans and trees.

From the perspective of mortal living beings, a primal spiritual image is the Tree as Universal Axis, which defines and unites the worlds and Realms. The Axis is most easily and directly encountered in the MiddleRealm, for the landscape itself provides or reveals thresholds, doorways and access points to and from the OverRealm and UnderRealm. At the same time, the mortal world is the place of regeneration and renewal, of expression and containment of Life. It is the central sphere of human life, the place that bridges and opens up the OtherWorld and other Realms.

Thus high places in the landscape are where the OverRealm is particularly accessible; low places give entrance to the UnderRealm, while centralised places (meadows, gardens, plains, islands, caves in mountains, glades in forests, etc.) give entrance to a regenerated vision of the landscape and the Three Realms as a whole.

The renewal of life energies that comes from meaningful spiritual participation in the turning of the seasonal cycles is also tightly knotted into the mystery of mortal reality.[11]

9 The Moon 🌙

To live with the Moon is to live with the cycles of change and renewal. Over approximately fourteen days the Moon weaves itself into being across the sky until it is full and shining. Then, over another 13 or 14 days, it unravels into nothing, disappears, then reappears two or three days later to begin the cycle again.

The Moon's "death," its three days of darkness, links it to the realm of the ancestors, to the UnderRealm within or below the Earth. The Moon has been called "the first of the dead," for it embodies and reveals the life and death cycle we are all living within. The Moon cycle thus contains a gate to the UnderRealm and the mysteries of renewal and ancestral power.

The Moon cycle also links to the rhythms of the tides and the menses, in other words, to the flux and reflux of the primal fluids of water and blood, and thus to the foundational powers of life. This connection with woman and the sea is, of course, also an interweaving with the Earth, the expresser or manifestation place of universal cycles and rhythms.

Figure 23: In esoteric lore, the Moon is known as the "first of the dead," for it reflects, in its monthly cycle the life rhythm of mortal beings: it is born out of darkness, grows to maturity and fullness, wanes and then dies, disappearing, only to be reborn again in an unending pattern. In archaic and traditional cultures the moon is perceived as being of the Night, and so is closely connected to nocturnal creatures, in particular the Owl. Above: *Owl Lady of the Night*— hand-painted on wood by Jessie Skillen 2013

The Full Moon appears about the same size as the Sun and thus is its partner, often rising in the East as the Sun sets in the West. In the interplay of their rhythms the Moon and Sun become one, unified, at the dark Moon in the UnderRealm. The seasonal cycle of the Sun and monthly cycle of the Moon also combine to give us the yearly cycle of the Lunar Wheel (12-13 lunar cycles within a seasonal solar cycle).

One of the unique features of the Moon is that it has a definite texture when viewed with the naked eye ~ and figures are easily envisioned in that texture. Most often in

sacred lore we find a rabbit (or hare) and a human face associated with the texture of the Moon. These are expressions of fecundity and ancestral power respectively.

8 Mercury ☿

The most noticeable characteristic of this planet is its elusiveness. Mercury is always close to the Sun and is visible only as a morning or evening star, by which it can be said to express manifesting dual or twin powers. It appears to dart from side to side of the Sun, rising and descending across the horizon frequently. It is thus closely linked to the passage of light in and out of the UnderRealm. Mercury's movements in relation to the Sun, Venus, and the horizon form a kind of dynamic crossroads pattern, and to an extent express the power of pattern making itself.

a. Sunrise ~ before Sun in East: Ascending, beginning, initiating energies of inspiration, valuation, feeling. Artistic perception, poetry.(feeling)

b. Sunset ~ behind Sun in West: Descending, waning, completing energies of reflection (thought)

Mercury can be seen to sparkle along the horizon (where the atmosphere is dense), which associates it with the idea of magical "brilliance" or

Figure 24: Cernunnos flanked by the Romano-Celtic deities Apollo and Mercury. Apollo signifies the planet mercury as a morning star and the god mercury the same planet as an evening star. Most interesting here is the appearance of Cernunnos seemingly as the sun itself or perhaps the UnderRealm sun at

splendour ~ the shining of the Inner Light.

7 Venus ♀

Venus shines brighter and more beautifully than any other planet, and thus embodies the power of attraction. Sharp-eyed observers would see that Venus has a horned phase, like the Moon, which links it both to the feminine mysteries of containment and to creative or sexual energy (The images are those of a vessel or cauldron and the horns of a cow, bull or stag).

Venus resonates with the Moon in other ways too. Like the Moon, it grows brighter the further it is from the Sun, and it is sometimes visible in the day sky. Also, Venus is visible for about nine months at a time, which links it to the human gestation cycle and the mysteries of becoming.

On the other hand, like Mercury, Venus is a morning and evening star and thus closely associated with the threshold of the horizon and

Figure 25: *The Planet Venus is often perceived as embodying a female or horned deity, an so has resonance to the moon. Venus is striking, beautiful, and always in relatively close proximity to the sun. Venus too is both a morning and evening star and, in sacred lore, is often associated with the sea. Inset: Venus, The MorningStar, rising over the sea.*

the coming and going of light and dark:

a. Sunrise ~ before Sun in East: Ascending energies of attraction (passion, desire)

b. Sunset ~ behind Sun in West: Descending energies of completion (sensation)

6 Sun ☉

The Sun dominates the sky in the day and hence expresses the powers of sovereignty and centrality.

The Sun's daily cycle is the governing rhythm of life on Earth. For human beings it also came early to reveal or embody an initiatory pattern which interweaves with and complements that of the Moon. For whereas the Moon is the revealer of the mystery of becoming, of light regenerating and growing out of darkness, the Sun reveals the mystery of being. The Sun does not diminish, die and regenerate like the Moon. It stays the same, emerging whole out of darkness at dawn, in the same form as when it entered at dusk.

There is thus a striking duality in the solar cycle — the primordial duality of light and darkness. This is not a matter of good and evil or light and

unlight, but more like within and without. Magical research at sacred sites indicates that some ancient peoples experienced night as the time when the Sun is active within the Earth. 4 Awareness of this primal solar duality is at the root of practices related to the Mystery of the Riven Sun.[12] In any event, these practices comprise a specialised form of magical work involving the

THREE NATURAL SUNS IN THE WORLD

Figure 26:*The Three Suns*, a pattern known from Rosicrucian texts of the seventeenth century,derives from ancient perceptions of the apparent birth and death of the solar disk each day. These perceptions are encapsulated in the esoteric Mystery of the Riven or Cloven Sun: The bright sun that illumines the day is cloven at dusk to shine deep beneath the earth at night. The point of mediation and harmony of these two secret lights is the mortal heart. For a useful practical discussion of the Three Suns see RJ Stewart, *The Miracle Tree (Career Press, NJ, 2003),esp. Chapter 4.*
Above. illustration from *Secret symbols of the Rosicrucians of the 16th & 17th Centuries — Altona 1785*

mediation of alternating magical rhythms (Suns) into a third reconciling centre. This third "Sun" manifests within the human form as a radiating inner light. In sacred lore this manifestation or epiphany is normally expressed in the myths and legends of saviour figures and sacred kings and queens.[13]

5 Mars ♂

Mars glows red like blood and fire. It appears suddenly, though regularly, in the sky and has an energetic, uncertain rhythm of movement. Back and forth along the ecliptic it goes, as though dancing or manoeuvring. This intricate patterning of movement resonates with the universal magical form of the labyrinth, which, in its most archaic style, resonates in turn with a primal magical weapon — the double-headed axe (or labrys). Like Jupiter and Saturn, Mars is visible in the night sky for long periods and of the three so-called "outer planets" it moves quickest.

Mars' brightness changes in intensity, making it seem to pulsate or send out potent streams of energy.

Its resonance with blood and fire links the planet to life death, destruction, war

civilisation (warmth, hearth fires), and sexuality (the inner fire).

Though not bound to the Sun like Venus and Mercury, Mars' attributes of heat and flame do link it to the Solar Wheel, as does its two-year cycle (two solar rotations) through the zodiac.

4 Jupiter ♃

Other than Venus and the Moon, Jupiter is the brightest light in the night sky. Unlike Venus, however, Jupiter stays in the sky for long periods and is sometimes visible at midnight.

Its height and unchanging brightness link it to the powers of rulership and sovereignty, which it shares, after a different fashion, with the Sun. This relationship is strengthened by its twelve-year cycle thorough the Zodiac, which extends and is mirrored in the twelve month solar/lunar cycle.

Its position as the central outer visible planet, between Mars and Saturn, marks is it as expressing the power that mediates or gives.

Figure 26 *The night sky is transcendent, luminous,* and awesome. *Above,* the Milky Way shines like a luminous River or a mighty Tree of Light or even a great mantle or cloak of stars. Insets: . In some streams of Sacred Lore, such as the Egyptian(left inset, the Star deity is female, while in others, like the Greco-Roman Uranos (right inset:) the deity is male.

3 Saturn ♄

Saturn is the slowest and farthest away of the visible planets ~ a fact that signifies limits or boundaries of time and space, and expresses the power of enfoldment.

Its remoteness also connects it to primordial times, that is, to fundamental things, basic forms and expressions of creation. Geometrically, Saturn could be symbolized by a triangle, which is the first possible form, yet also has connections with woman, birth and the creative structure of the Universe (The Three Realms).

Saturn's cycle of 28 years is a resonance or octave of the lunar cycle of 28 days. Thus in some sense Saturn holds a similar magical relationship to the Moon and Jupiter does to the Sun.

2 Sky & Stars ✸

The Sky is transcendent, luminous, and awesome. At night it is as a sea or blanket of stars. Yet patterns and movements are discernible amidst the shining mantle. These include the constellations,

the Milky Way and outstanding phenomena such as shooting stars, comets and meteors, some of which fell to earth and became sacred objects. Meteoric iron and other rocks fallen from the sky support a unified inner vision: the stars above and Earth below are conjoined, the Realms are united.

Figure 28: **Weaver of Destiny** *by William Blake*

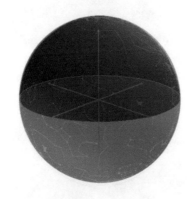

Figure 27: Celestial Sphere.

Among the constellations, the band of the Zodiac stands apart as marking the pathway along which the Sun, Moon and planets wander in their courses. Also markedly obvious is the path or stream that crosses the Zodiac at the (current) points of equinox and solstice ~ the Milky Way. These two great bands have long functioned as magical or rivers that can be traveled in Vision to the Otherworld. At the same time they embody initiatory patterns of regenerative, rotational energies.

Other constellations, especially those that circle the poles seem to open a spiral way in and out of the celestial sphere.

The Three Wheels & the Planets

The forms and rhythms of The Magical Tree fall naturally into three rotational patterns:

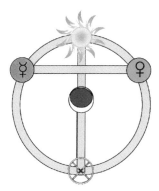

One: *The Lunar Wheel,* centred on the Moon ☽ is concerned with the cycle of becoming: Foundational rhythms of life and time, the spiralling cycles of birth, growth, age, death and rebirth...
are expressed in humans, plants, animals, ancestors and all other living creatures (⊕ Earth) ...
that exchange life energies through patterns of consciousness (☿Mercury)...
and emotional force (♀ Venus).

These rhythms culminate in, or contain, the promise of wholeness of being and liberation from fragmented perceptions of reality (☉Sun).

Figure 29a: Stylised variant of Lunar Wheel

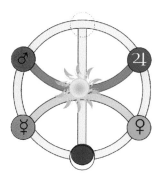

Two: The Solar Wheel, centred on the Sun ☉, and expressing the power of being, is a holism that balances or harmonises energies. For example:
♂ Mars , removal and regeneration, **balances with**
♃ Jupiter , flow and bestowal;
♀ Venus, attraction and completion, *harmonises with*
☿ Mercury, inspiration (brilliance) and reflection;
☽ Moon, fulfilment through foundational or sexual energies (on deeper magical levels this relates to the raising of the dragon or serpent fire), *balances with*
Void, ◉ opening connections to the Unknown, which is beyond duality.

1 & 0 The Pivot ✳ & The Void ◉

The stars seem fixed to a great sphere or dome of dark light that is revolving, turning on an axis which runs north-south through the Earth. This great spindle magically binds the planets and stars together, weaving the mystery of destiny into the earthly cycles of life and death.

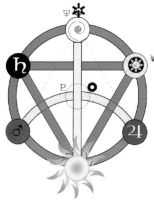

Three: The Stellar Wheel, centred on the Void or Mystery ◉, is concerned with thresholds of being and non-being: From the Unknown, the source of universal creation and destruction, the mystery of regeneration bursts into being as ... outpouring or streaming universal power (Stars ✲); enfolded into time, space and primal form (♄ Saturn); actively giving itself to building more complex forms (♃ Jupiter); or breaking down forms into essential energies (♂ Mars);

in harmony with the cycles of the Sun and planets; and with the rotation or precession of the Great Year (✳ pivot).

It will be noted that several of the star forms

(☉, ☽, ☿, ♀, ♃, ♄, ♇, ◉) appear

in more than one Wheel. This interweaving of the Wheels is an expression of ongoing, organic interchanges of energy among the Earth, the Sun, Moon, planets and stars. The common factor in all three Wheels is the Sun. This should not surprise, as the Sun is a physical anchor for all centralising, harmonising spiritual forces.

27

Here also is the power of universal regeneration. The rotation of the celestial axis and changing position of the pivot, which sometimes points to a specific star (such as Polaris in the current epoch), yet for the most part of its revolution points to a dark spot — a vertical or virtual void — express great universal cycles of regeneration, creation, and destruction.

In many archaic and esoteric traditions the celestial Pole or Pivot is envisioned as holding the tent or arch of the universe in place, while simultaneously allowing access to the reality beyond the stars. This latter may be experienced as a universal sea of light, an ocean of ultimate or infinite being, or as an endless void of non-being.

Practices:

Awareness of cosmic rhythms.

Most magicians in the industrialised West are shamefully out of tune with the rhythms of the planets and stars. The first step in re-orienting to cosmic rhythms is to learn to look. Look at the landscape around you, even if this is a city park or your own back yard; find east, west, south and north; see the high places and the low places; view a sunrise or (more likely) a sunset; seek out the Moon; look up at the stars. You can locate various constellations by referencing books, however, by far the easiest and most effective way of orienting yourself to the sky is with the aid of one of the many planetarium programs available for your home computer. It only takes a few minutes each night under a clear sky to become familiar with the patterns, motions and rhythms of the Stars, Moon and planets. Learn one constellation each night by finding it on your planetarium program or in your star chart book, then going outside and locating it in the sky. Start with the more visible ones like Orion and the Great Bear. Focus on the 42 ancient constellations (see magicalways.com for a list), as these have long traditions of sacred lore rooted in esoteric work. In a few weeks (weather permitting) you should know most of them.

A good exercise is to use your planetarium program to look at the pattern of the sky around your birth date and year. Look at the night before and after you were born, see what was happening at sunrise or sunset. See which planets and stars were above the horizon, and which were below. Find the moon phase.

Do the same for today. If you are familiar with modern astrology, you may be surprised how different things are in real time and space compared to the mathematical and generally abstracted pattern of the standard tropical astrology chart (for instance you'll be able to see planets in constellations in the sky — ironically, a rare experience among horoscopists today). Spend a minute or two meditating on the great holism of Sky, Earth and living mortal creatures. Realise your place within this holism and its place within you.

Raising the Axis

Standing:

Be aware of the land around you. Feel the Earth beneath your feet and the fire at the centre of the planet. Draw light up from the centre of the Earth into your body.

28

Now become aware of the Moon in the sky and feel it resonating with the bio-psychic centre at your genitals and root of your spine. See and sense a Moon (this should be in the phase the Moon was at your birth) building in this area of your body. Sense this Moon going thorough its phases within you.

Next be aware of the Sun in the sky. Feel it activating your heart, then see and sense a Sun there, illuminating you from within.

Now see the stars revolving in the sky and be aware of a star shining from your brow.

Feel the stellar light opening up your powers of seership and utterance. Be aware of your breathing, and of the pause between breaths signifying the Divine Void. Feel your throat opening up and utter the sacred vowels O-U-I-E-A as you see and sense a stream of light running vertically from earth to stars through the sensitive points in your body. As the call fades away so does the vision of the streaming Axis and centres end, and you return to mundane awareness.

Opening the Three Wheels

The following Practices may be done individually or together.

i

Be aware of the Sun, realise how its journey bestows day and night upon the Earth, how its binary rhythm interacts with living beings in the landscape. Flowers open at dawn, sleeping creatures awaken and begin their daily activities. Then at dusk, the flowers begin to close, and creatures prepare for rest and sleep. At night the Sun is beneath the Earth, and its secret, invisible light is accessible within the deeps of the land. Feel the Sun cycle repeating itself over and over in a rhythm of timeless, unending alternation of light and dark ~ a state of simply "being."

ii

Next become aware of the lunar rhythm. Sense the cycle of becoming expressed in the Moon's phases: birth, growth, fullness, decline and death. Be aware of the interaction of the Moon and the Sun and how this generates the flow of time, the cycle or spiral of the year measured in months and seasons upon the Earth. Realise how this in turn opens a sense of historical or progressive time, now recognisable in years and phases of development.

iii

Now focus on stellar cycles. See and sense the great wheeling of the stars overhead, which provides a local measure of time and a means of orientation at night. Be aware also how the star patterns are slowly changing, releasing great forces of cosmic regeneration as the Earth transits from one epoch to another. Feel your place in the present time as a spiritual mediator on the threshold of one such Great Turning.

When ready, return to daily awareness.

Enfolding the Three Wheels

These more advanced practices are examples of empowerment through enfoldment. Enfoldment is where you merge your body and personal space or energy field with a magical form or pattern — in this case the Three Wheels. The reversing of the Axes are singled out as important thresholds in the Visions.

The Wheel visions can be built individually over several sessions (for the less experienced) or all at once. It

is important that as you envision each magical sign, you consciously link to its corresponding star form in the sky. For an explanation of the Magical use of Colour, see Folio III Signs, Resonances and Forms.

i

Standing:

Build the Lunar Wheel of Personal Becoming around you:

Feel the Moon ☽ at your genitals, see and sense it passing through its phases.

Connect to the Earth-Fire in the centre of the planet;

And to the Sun in your heart.

To your right side, in line with your right hip see and sense, in brilliant orange light, the magical sign of Mercury☿;

To your left side, lined up with your left hip see and sense, in vivid green, the magical sign of Venus♀;

Rotate the Wheel clockwise so that the Earth-Fire is in your Heart, The Sun in the Earth, and Mercury and Venus are reversed. Return the Wheel to its initial position.

ii

Standing:

Build the Solar Wheel of Transpersonal Being:

Feel the Sun in your heart;

And the Moon in your genitals;

Focus on your throat and note the pause between breaths ~ the opening of the power of the Void.

In brilliant orange to your right, on a level with your hip, is the magical sign of Mercury ☿;

To your left hip, in green, is the magical sign of Venus ♀;

To your right side, line up with your right shoulder, in deep royal blue, is the magical sign of Jupiter ♃;

To the left, in line with your left shoulder, and glowing fiery red, is the magical sign of Mars ♂;

Reach out with your left and right hands and touch the various forms in pairs, feeling their complementary energies flowing through your arms and harmonising within your heart.

Rotate the Wheel clockwise 180 degrees and harmonise the powers.

Return the Solar Wheel to its initial position.

iii

Standing:

Envision the Stellar Wheel of Transcendent Regeneration.

Focus on your throat centre and on your breathing, realising the pause between breaths as a threshold point that opens onto the Great Mystery, the Divine Void.

See and sense the Sun within your heart and feel a point of light above your head, like a bright jewel.

To your right and left, aligned with your shoulders, are the magical signs of Mars ♂ and Jupiter ♃ in their corresponding colours.

Above them, in line with your temples, are the magical signs of Saturn ♄, to the right and black in colour; and the Sky ✪ which is silvery, stardust gray.

Rotate the Wheel counterclockwise, meditating briefly on each form as it moves into position above your head. Pause when the Wheel is reversed and the Sun is above and the Pivot below. When the full cycle is complete, end the Practice and return to daily consciousness.

Notes

1 Page 5. I have employed the spelling Qabala in this folio as it is in alignment with the "science of letters" which plays a large role in traditional Qabalistic thought. The english letters QBL share the same predecessors as their Hebrew counterparts. The modern conventional spelling "Kabbalah" now in common usage is it seems to me, to be avoided as it seems to have arisen as an effort by modern academics, to supplant the esoteric significance of the word with one that is, at best, a pandering to "phonetics"and at worst, an attempt (likely unconscious) to alter the energetic meaning of the tradition itself.

2 Page 6. Mircea Eliade, *Shamanism: Archaic Techniques of Ecstasy.* Princeton University Press (January 19, 2004).

3 Page 6. Simo Parpola The Assyrian Tree of Life: Tracing the Origins of Jewish Monotheism and Greek Philosophy, JNES 52 no.3, 1993

4 Page 6. Don Karr *The Study of Christian Cabala in English,* available for viewing online at digital-brilliance.com/kab/karr/index.htm

5 Page 7. Nor do I suggest that the Three Wheels model derives from modern heliocentric cosmology. On the other hand, focusing on the primal rhythms and integral meanings of planets, stars, and luminaries lets us see why particular star forms resonate with certain traditions and deities. However, resonance does not imply identification, despite the unfortunate and widespread tendency of esotericists, occultists and Qabalists to confuse deities with planets. This is itself the symptom of a greater malaise ~ the occult obsession with "attributions." Such morbid fascinations are behind the rather fatuous descriptions of the Magical Tree as a "card-index filing system" or "primitive computer."

6 Page 12. *The Book of Formation* or *Sephir Yetzirah* is available in translation in many editions, printed and online.

7 Page 19. "What is now known as Glastonbury was, in medieval times, called the Isle of Avalon. It is virtually an island, for it is completely surrounded by marshlands. In Welsh it is called Ynys Afallach, which means the Island of Apples." Gerald of Wales, *Liber de Principis instructione* c.1193

8 page 19 It is lso worth noting the etymology of the word Astronomy: *Gr.. astro = star or planet, luminous body + nomos = ordinance, song, tradition.*

9 Page 21. Archaic and esoteric tradition universally acknowledges a pattern of Three Realms or regions of the cosmos. The Three Realms are OverRealm, MidRealm, and UnderRealm. These resonate with the ancient threefold Celtic pattern of Sky, Land and Sea (Sea including here the molten Sea of lava within the earth and the Ocean of stars around it).
Briefly speaking, the OverRealm is everything above the horizon, the UnderRealm everything below the horizon and the MidRealm includes the topography and atmosphere within the circle of the horizon. Horizon, however, includes the horizon (or limitations) of one's consciousness as well as that of the visible landscape.

10 Page 21. The Two Worlds are :
 The Mortal World where spiritual energies "manifest" – it is our physical reality as vehicle of Spirit. The manifest world is not as is often taught the lowest point on a scale of existence, but rather the central point – a place of mediation between all Worlds, Realms and Directions.
The OtherWorld, which is the world of spirit that exists in parallel to our own mortal world. The OtherWorld contains presences and powers that enable the Mortal World to become "paradisal" or whole.

11 Page 22. Mortal reality is characterised by thresholds, the most significant of is the threshold of life and death,upon which which is founded much in magico-spiritual and initatic traditions.

12 Page 24. "Your two wheels, Surya, the Brahmins know in their measured rounds. But the one wheel that is hidden, only the inspired know that." (*Rg Veda* 10.85- 16)
Surya is an ancient deity linked to the Sun. The first two wheels are the diurnal (primary Solar) and annual (Lunar) Wheels. The hidden wheel is the (Stellar) Wheel of the Great Year, which marks changing epochs of spiritual,
magical energy.
For the Three Suns in Rosicrucian traditions, see Manley P Hall's *Secret Teaching of All Ages*, LI, "The Three Suns" and the anonymous chapbook *Secret symbols of the Rosicrucians of the 16th & 17th Centuries* ~Altona 1785
The esoterically important Jewish cosmological text Sepher Yetzirah presents the Sun, Moon, planets and stars (zodiac) in terms of three interlacing wheels or rings. Previously obscure references in the text (i.e. the dragon, the sphere or circle and the heart) attain new meaning when looked at in relation to lunar, stellar and solar cycles. (See above, note 6)
It is also worth noting that in some schools of occult Qabala, the planets are given the seemingly bizarre title "Mundane Chakras" ~ simply meaning "Planetary (or Earthly) Wheels."

13 Page 24. Like a child's top, the Earth not only spins, it wobbles, which means that its axis moves in a circle through the heavens. From the point of view of Earth this makes the pivot point of the stars slowly change position over millennia. A full cycle of movement takes approximately 26,000 years and is known as a Platonic Year or a Great Year

About The Author

Coleston Brown enjoys a simple life in the Irish countryside. He spends most of his free time quietly working on various projects designed to further the Faery-Human Covenant and the Magical Way.

www. magicalways.com

Picture Credits

Pages 2-32, Celtic Knot page runner © 1997 by Jessie Skillen.

Page 1: *The Magical Tree* © Coleston Brown 2013

Page 5

Figure 1: The Magical Tree © Coleston Brown 2013

Figure 2: Redrawn version of the drawing of a shaman's drum made on a 1909-1913 expedition led by Anokhin Andrei Viktorovich, published in 1924 in *Materialy po shamanstvy u altaitsev* ("materials on the shamanism of the Altai people"). Image in the Public Domain.

Figure 3: Portae Lucis by Joseph Gikatilla (1248-1325) Augsburg, 1516. Image in the Public Domain.

Page 6

Figure 4: mesopotamian Cylindar seal courtesy British Museum

Figure 5 Sotdae, Shamanic Poles. Photo by Hjmin 2008. Public Domain

Figure 6 Three Wheel Tree from *Secret symbols of the Rosicrucians of the 16th & 17th Centuries ~Altona 1785*

Page 8

Figures 7a, b, c & 8 Three Wheels Magical Tree © Coleston Brown 2013

Page 9

Figure 9: Magical Tree with numbered Paths. © Coleston Brown 2013

Figure 10: Dundon Yew. Photo courtesy of Robert Henry.

Page 10

Figure11: From Kircher's *Œdipus Ægypticus* published in 1652. Image in the Public Domain.

Figure 12: Modern version of Qabalistic Tree. Picture by Rodrigotebani. Image in the Public Domain.

Page 11

Figure 13: detail from the North High Cross at Aheny.

Figure 14: Bird Shaman, Lascaux circa 17000 BP. Image in the Public Domain.

Page 13

Figure 15: Jack and the Beanstalk

illustration by Walter Crane *(1845–1915)*. Image in the Public Domain.

Figure 16: Mithraic Mydteries. Photo courtesy Vassil. Image in the Public Domain.

Figure 17: Jacob's Ladder by William Blake. Painted c. 1800. Image in the Public Domain.

Pages 14-15

Figures 18a-e & 18 f-h: How to Draw the Magical Tree © Coleston Brown 2013.

Page 16

Figure 19 Seahenge. Photo courtesy of John Sayer www.sayer.abel.co.uk.

Page 17

Figure 2o: Ballinagree menhir, County Cork, Ireland photo by Ceoil. Image in the Public Domain.
inset: Deer Stone in Mongolia photo courtesy Marissa Smith 2007. Image licensed under the Creative Commons Attribution 2.0 Generic license.

Figure 21: The Star, painting © Coleston Brown 2008.

Page 18

Figure 22: The Oak King and The Holly King painting © Jessie Skillen, 1994.

Page 22:

Figure 23 Owl, Lady of the Night~hand painted on wood © Jessie Skillen 2013

Figure 24: Cernunnos flanked by the Romano-Celtic deities Apollo and Mercury. Image in the Public Domain.

Mercury.

Page 23

Figure 25: The Mermaid painting by Howard Pyle 1910. *inset: Venus, The MorningStar, rising over the sea* photo bt BillC,2008. Image in the Public Domain.

Page 25

Figure 26: The MilkyWay. Photo by Jurvetson (flickr)
Insets: *left: The Goddess Nuit* photo by Golden Meadows,2006. Public Domain. Right *Aion-Uranus with Terra (Greek Gaia)* on mosaic photo by Bibi Saint-Pol 2007. Image in the Public Domain.

Page 26

Figure 27: Celestial Sphere © Coleston Brown 2013.

Figure 28: Weaver of Destiny by William Blake. Painted c. 1800 Image in the Public Domain.

Page 27

Figures 29-31: Three Wheels Magical Tree © Coleston Brown 2013.

Pages 28, 31: Green Man painting © Jessie Skillen, 1994.

Page 33: The Oak King and The Holly King painting © Jessie Skillen, 1994.

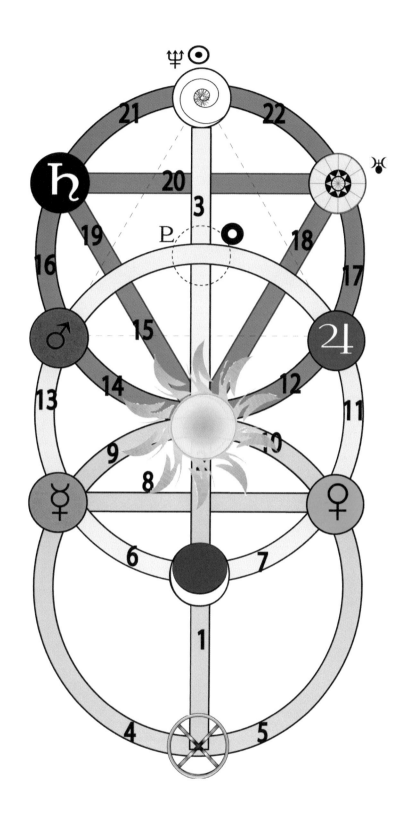